W9-CNC-183

EXAMINING
SHIPWRECKS

BY HAYDEN WEDGE

CLARA
HOUSE
BOOKS

First published in 2015 by Clara House Books, an imprint of
The Oliver Press, Inc.

Clara House Books
5707 West 36th Street
Minneapolis, MN 55416
USA

Editors: Mirella Miller and Arnold Ringstad
Series Designer: Maggie Villaume

Picture Credits
Getty Images News/Thinkstock, cover, 1; Hyung Min-Woo/Yonhap/AP Images, 4; Yonhap/
AP Images, 7; Thinkstock, 8; Vincent St. Thomas/Shutterstock Images, 11; Nils Bergslien,
12; Library of Congress, 15; Dorling Kindersley/Thinkstock, 17; Shutterstock Images, 18; US
National Archives and Records Administration, 20; Richard Schlecht/National Geographic
Society/Corbis, 23; Harry Trask/AP Images, 25; Michael Stubblefield/iStock/Thinkstock, 27;
Durden Images/Shutterstock Images, 28; Rick Naystatt/US Navy, 31; Salvatore Conte/iStock/
Thinkstock, 32–33; Petty Officer 3rd Class Stephen Lehmann/US Coast Guard, 36; Petty Officer
3rd Class Robert Brazzell/US Coast Guard, 38; Petty Officer 3rd Class Kevin J. Neff/US Coast
Guard, 40–41

Every attempt has been made to clear copyright. Should there be any inadvertent omission,
please apply to the publisher for rectification.

Library of Congress Cataloging-in-Publication Data

Wedge, Hayden, author.
  Examining shipwrecks / by Hayden Wedge.
     pages cm – (Examining disasters)
  Includes index.
  Audience: 7 to 8.
  ISBN 978-1-934545-67-6 (hardcover : alk. paper) – ISBN 978-1-934545-83-6 (ebook)
  1. Shipwrecks–Juvenile literature. I. Title. II. Series: Examining disasters.

  G525.W34 2015
  910.4'52–dc23

                                   2014044476

Printed in the United States of America
CG1022015

www.oliverpress.com

CONTENTS

ONE

THE *SEWOL* FERRY DISASTER

On April 16, 2014, a ferry carrying 476 people sank off the coast of South Korea on its way to Jeju, a popular island destination. More than two-thirds of the passengers were students from Danwon High School on a field trip. The disaster ultimately claimed the lives of 304 passengers.

The *Sewol* ferry departed from Incheon, South Korea, at 9:00 p.m. on April 15. The overnight trip to Jeju was 300 miles (400 km) long and would take more than 13 hours. It was a well-traveled route that the *Sewol* completed three times each week.

The South Korean coast guard attempts to rescue passengers of the sunken *Sewol* ferry.

MISTAKES

At exactly 8:48 a.m., the *Sewol* made a sharp turn. This may have resulted from the ship striking a rock or other underwater obstacle. The turn likely caused the ferry's cargo to shift, putting the ship off balance. The *Sewol* was carrying 3,608 tons (3,273 metric tons) of cargo when it sank, which is three times as much as it could safely carry.

A junior officer, not the more experienced captain, was steering the ship when it began to tip to one side. The younger officer had never sailed those waters before, and the captain was not there to supervise her. The area where the *Sewol* sank has many islands close together. Fast currents make the waters difficult to navigate. At 8:55 a.m., the *Sewol* crew sent out a distress signal. As the ship tipped further to the left, water began to pour into the main cabin.

Helicopters fly over the sinking Korean ship as rescuers try to reach the trapped passengers.

EVACUATION

The captain and crew made mistakes that contributed to the tragedy. The captain did not give an order for the passengers to evacuate the ferry because rescue ships had not yet arrived. He worried that the strong currents and cold waters would place the passengers in danger.

The captain told passengers to stay in their rooms when the *Sewol* began tipping. They were not moved to evacuation points to await the arrival of rescue ships. An

8:55 a.m.
First distress signal
sent out from the crew

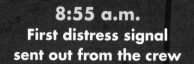

9:30 a.m.
Coast guard ships
and helicopters start
arriving; ferry tilted
60 degrees

9:45 a.m.
First helicopter
rescue

10:00 a.m.
Ongoing helicopter rescue from
upturned side; rescues take place
from overturned side

11:20 a.m.
The ferry is
submerged

SINKING OF THE *SEWOL*

The *Sewol* began to tilt after a sudden turn. Study the diagram of the *Sewol*'s tipping. How might this angle have made it more difficult to rescue passengers? Why might passengers trapped in the lower decks have had a harder time escaping once the *Sewol* began to tilt?

evacuation order was finally issued 30 minutes after the ship began tipping. According to the crew, the *Sewol* had tilted 60 degrees to the left, making it impossible for the passengers to move throughout the ferry. When the waters began pouring in, passengers were trapped in their rooms. The *Sewol* did not have enough life jackets for all of the passengers, and only two of its forty lifeboats were used to move passengers to safety.

Between 9:30 a.m. and 11:00 a.m., helicopters and nearby boats rescued the passengers and crew who were able to escape, including the captain and the junior officer. At 11:20 a.m., the *Sewol* was submerged.

AFTERMATH OF THE SHIPWRECK

Crew members were arrested days after the sinking. They were charged with not performing their duties and failing to help passengers in need. Four crew members,

DANGERS DURING RECOVERY

Strong currents and poor water conditions hampered the rescue and recovery operation following the sinking of the *Sewol*. Divers first looked for survivors by tapping on the hull, or outside surface, of the ship and listening for a response, but they soon began looking for bodies rather than survivors. Many bodies were difficult to access because of locked doors and debris. Two divers died in recovery operations after losing consciousness underwater. Rescuers must weigh the chances of finding survivors against the risks to divers when planning a rescue operation.

including the captain and the junior officer, were charged with murder.

Anger at the government's response to the disaster forced South Korean Prime Minister Chung Hong-won to resign, but President Park Geun-hye remained in office. President Park disbanded South Korea's coast guard for its poor response to the disaster and recovery. The former coast guard duties were to be given to a newly created Department for National Safety. The worst South Korean maritime disaster in 20 years had far-reaching effects on the country and its people. Maritime experts around the world took steps to prevent similar disasters in the future.

TWO

HOW SHIPS FLOAT

As long as people have traveled by sea, ships have crashed. For thousands of years, people built boats for fishing, travel, and trade. The oldest shipwreck ever found dates back to 2200 BCE, more than 4,200 years ago! It lies near the coast of Greece. There are likely many older shipwrecks that have not been found. People settled islands, such as Australia, tens of thousands of years ago. Some of these settlers' ships likely sank, but these early wrecks have broken down, making them difficult or impossible to find.

In the days before airplanes and cars, ships were the only way to travel to certain places. Mountain ranges were hard to cross by foot or on horseback, and robbers attacked travelers on land.

The ancient Vikings fought many battles at sea. Their boats likely lie on the ocean floor today.

DUGOUT CANOES

Dugouts are canoe-like boats made from a single hollowed-out log. They are among the oldest boats archaeologists have discovered. Some dugouts date back to the Stone Age, more than 10,000 years ago. Broken dugouts were fixed using clay to prevent sinking. Dugouts were used around the world. They sailed on rivers and oceans, and were used to travel and to fish.

Travel by sea had its own dangers. Early ships sank for many reasons, including poor design, storms, overloading, warfare, fire, and attacks by pirates. Ships also lacked good maps and navigational tools, which caused them to strike rocks or reefs.

SAILING TECHNOLOGY

As explorers ventured farther into the world's seas and oceans in the 1500s, sailing technology improved. Still, early ships were largely limited to the winds that pushed their sails as their source of movement. Steamships were used in the 1800s. Unlike previous vessels, steamships did not need wind to move them. Their steam power introduced some new problems, however. Furnace fires and boiler explosions, both part of the mechanism generating the steam, caused many disasters.

A steamship docks in Savannah, Georgia, in the early 1900s.

Modern ships run on diesel fuel and electricity. Sailors have accurate maps and high-tech tools to find their way. They can radio for help, and stricter safety laws have made ships safer as well. Despite these advances, shipwrecks still occur. Mistakes can be made, even with modern technology.

WEIGHT AND BUOYANCY

The shape of a boat and the weight it carries are important factors in whether it will float. What is the difference between the diagram in the middle and the diagram on the right? Why does the boat float while the raft sinks? Identify the keel, or the structure on the bottom of the boat. What might happen to this boat without the keel?

STAYING AFLOAT

It may be hard to imagine how an object weighing more than 52,000 tons (47,200 metric tons), such as the *Titanic*, can float. The ancient Greek scientist Archimedes figured out the basic science behind how ships float. Archimedes's principle explains the concept of buoyancy. The principle states the force pushing up on a ship is equal to the weight of water the ship pushes out of the way. In other words, the *Sewol* pushed 6,825 tons (6,192 metric tons) of water out of the way to stay afloat.

SEAORBITER

Boats have come a long way since dugout canoes. New boats continued to be developed. One next-generation vessel is called the SeaOrbiter. When it is built, it will be 190 feet (58 m) tall. Half of that height will permanently be below water, allowing scientists to conduct underwater research. The SeaOrbiter will drift with ocean currents and generate power from wind, sunlight, and waves.

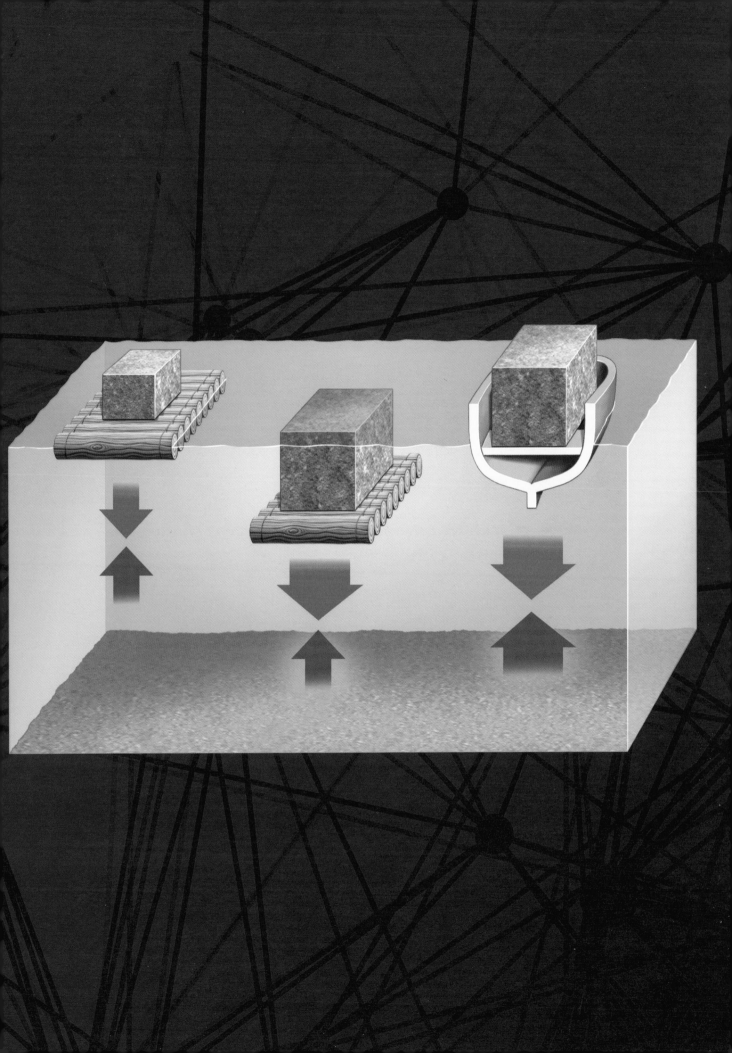

Modern ships have better technology and stronger structures to prevent and withstand accidents.

The secret to staying afloat is in the shape of an object. A solid block of metal would sink in water. But when the metal is stretched out and filled with air, it pushes water out of the way over a larger area. Distributing the weight like this allows a boat to float. Engineers use lightweight, sturdy materials to build ships. They must spread the weight of the ship evenly across its body, or hull.

A strong, straight keel keeps a ship stable. The hull of a large ship is often shaped like a large rectangle with rounded edges. These edges let the boat slide easily through the water. The rectangular hull is lower in the water than those ships with v shapes. A ship with a rectangular hull is less likely to tip over. Modern ships often have watertight compartments inside their hulls. These compartments can be sealed off if they start to flood, preventing water from spreading to the rest of the hull.

HOW SCIENCE WORKS
ARCHIMEDES'S PRINCIPLE

Archimedes of Syracuse lived in ancient Greece more than 2,200 years ago. He was a talented mathematician and inventor, and he made many important observations about water and buoyancy. The development of his theories began when King Hiero II asked Archimedes to figure out whether his crown was made of pure gold or not, without damaging it or melting it down. While taking a bath, Archimedes thought of a way to test this. He noticed the water rose and splashed out when he got into his bath. This led him to understand the basic concepts behind displacement, which he could use to measure volume.

Archimedes conducted an experiment. He carefully measured how much water the crown pushed out of the way when dropped in water. This displaced water gave him the exact volume of the crown. Archimedes then divided the weight of the crown by its volume to find its density. He discovered the crown's density was different than the known density of gold. This meant some cheaper metals had been added to the crown, and it was not pure gold. The finding led Archimedes to do more experiments and make more discoveries about buoyancy.

THREE

HOW SHIPS SINK

Many different factors can cause shipwrecks, but the most common reason is water entering the hull and sinking the ship. When the *Sewol* tipped, this allowed water to enter the vessel. In the case of the *Nuestra Señora de Atocha*, a jagged reef sliced a hole in its hull as it headed from Cuba to Spain in 1622. A storm drove the ship further into the reef. It quickly sank. The *Titanic* famously sank after running into an iceberg. In 2012, the cruise ship *Costa Concordia* sank after running into an obstacle in shallow water. Rarely, a collision with an animal can sink a ship. A sperm whale brought down the *Essex* in 1820. The ship was on a whale-hunting expedition when the whale rammed it. The impact tore open the ship's hull, and it soon sank.

When it started its first voyage, the *Titanic* was considered one of the safest, most modern ships in the world.

SHIPWRECKS DURING WAR

Many ships are intentionally sunk during wars. The deadliest shipwreck in history happened during World War II (1939–1945). In January 1945, a Soviet submarine sank the German ship *Wilhelm Gustloff*. Up to 9,400 military personnel and civilians died.

Not all ships are sunk by holes in their hulls, however. Powerful winds and an unstable design sunk the *Mary Rose* in 1545. This ship belonged to King Henry VIII of England. The ship's crew set out to fight the French navy in the English Channel, the body of water between England and mainland Europe. After firing its cannons on one side, the *Mary Rose* turned sharply to bring its guns around to the other side. A gust of wind caused the ship to tilt at a dramatic angle. The top of the ship was too heavy,

After it sank in the English Channel, the *Mary Rose* wreck was not discovered until 1971.

making it unstable in the sea. Water poured into its gun ports, and the *Mary Rose* sank.

OTHER SHIPWRECK CAUSES

Ships can also sink following collisions with each other. The Italian ship *Andrea Doria* sank in 1956 after colliding with another ship near the coast of Massachusetts. The fog made it hard to see clearly. Radar on both ships indicated that the other was nearby, but the crews were not well trained. They could not tell exactly how far away they were from the other. The other ship, the *Stockholm*, plowed into the side of the *Andrea Doria,* carving out a 30-foot (9-m) hole. After the disaster, radar training was improved.

Some ships sink because they are loaded too heavily. Their weight overpowers the buoyancy that keeps them afloat. For more revenue, shipping companies have sometimes overloaded their vessels. In the 1860s, British politician Samuel Plimsoll suggested that every ship should have lines on the hull showing when the ship was loaded to a safe level.

ROGUE WAVES

Sailors often told tales of giant waves measuring as high as 100 feet (30 m) that came out of nowhere and threatened to sink ships, but those stories were often dismissed as tall tales. Now radar satellites have confirmed the existence of rogue waves, which have been blamed for as many as 200 shipwrecks since the 1980s. Rogue waves occur when several factors, such as high winds and strong currents, join to create monster waves in deep seas. Rogue waves pose a danger to even the biggest ships.

Now laws require that ships not be loaded past these lines, often called Plimsoll lines. Overloading still occasionally happens. In 2012, the Russian cargo ship *Amurskaya* sank after being overloaded with gold ore. The *Swanland* sank in 2011 due to overloading and a rusty hull.

People sometimes sink old, unused ships on purpose to form artificial reefs. These make good fishing spots and interesting sites for scuba divers to visit. Workers remove oil and other chemicals from the old ship, take out valuable parts such as copper wiring, and cut openings

HOW SCIENCE WORKS
SHIPWRECKS AS PRESERVERS OF HISTORY

The evidence gathered by studying shipwrecks can change how scientists understand historical events. From recovered artwork, archaeologists knew the Minoans from the Mediterranean island of Crete were a seafaring people with many different types of ships, but archaeologists had never found a wreck of a Minoan ship. Then in 2003, archaeologists discovered pottery underwater near the coast of Crete that seemed to be from a small trading vessel. Archaeologists studied where the pottery lay on the seafloor, where the clay in the pots was from, and the different types of goods the ship carried. They were able to determine that the ship was probably a small vessel that stopped at different ports around the island to trade with locals. The wreck gave archaeologists a better understanding of how the Minoans traded goods.

Algae and other sea life grows on a shipwreck from the 1940s.

in the hull so divers can enter. After the ship has sunk, living things such as coral, barnacles, and algae grow on it and attract fish and other sea life.

FOUR

STUDYING SHIPWRECKS

In addition to understanding when and why ships sank, studying wrecked ships can teach us more about the people who sailed them. For example, dated bricks found on an unidentified wreck off the coast of Florida proved it could not have sunk before 1857.

The ocean is not kind to shipwrecks and the artifacts inside them. Waves, bacteria, sea animals, and ocean salts can damage wrecks. In some cases, however, cold temperatures and silt can protect items from decay. Fragile items such as postcards were found intact at the *Titanic* wreck site.

Archaeological divers can explore much deeper areas and stay underwater far longer than they could in the past.

MORE THAN ARCHAEOLOGY

Biologists also explore shipwrecks to learn more about deep-sea life. Many new types of sea life have been found this way, including deep-sea fish, bacteria, and worms. Scientists who discovered the *Titanic* learned that previously unknown iron-eating bacteria created rusty growths. These growths looked like icicles, leading scientists to name them *rusticles*.

DIVING TECHNOLOGY

The study of human activity related to the sea is known as maritime archaeology. This science has grown in the last 50 years as diving equipment has improved. Early divers used diving bells and clumsy helmets to salvage wrecks in shallow water. The first scuba equipment was invented in 1943, giving divers more freedom of movement. Now divers wear high-tech scuba gear and breathe special mixed gases that allow them to dive deeper and for longer time. To explore deeper still, people built undersea vehicles called submarines. Miniature submarines called submersibles take humans far below the surface. They can go much deeper than large submarines. Similar machines without people in them are called remotely operated vehicles (ROVs). They are connected to ships on the surface by

A U.S. Navy diver practices working with an autonomous underwater vehicle (AUV) in a pool.

cables and controlled by an operator on the ship. ROVs carry cameras and robotic arms. They explore shipwrecks without putting humans in danger. Autonomous underwater vehicles (AUVs) are robot submarines with no cables. They are programmed to follow a certain path underwater and return to the ship.

Sponsons, the large white boxes on the damaged ship's sides, helped the *Costa Concordia* float during salvage operations.

GATHERING CLUES

Although some divers grab every artifact in sight, professional archaeologists take a different approach.

Before touching an underwater site, they draw detailed maps that include natural features, such as cliffs, caves, and reefs. They also take photographs before carefully excavating, or digging out, the site. This is painstaking

PARBUCKLING AND REFLOATING

To salvage the *Costa Concordia* wreck, engineers turned to a process known as parbuckling. Salvage operators rotated the *Costa Concordia* upright, because it was lying on its side. Since the ship was full of water, it would not float on its own. Operators built an underwater platform for the ship to rest on. Big box-like structures called sponsons were attached to the sides of the *Costa Concordia*. This added enough buoyancy that the ship could float again and be towed away for salvage.

work. Divers use hammers and picks to remove mud and rock. Then they fan the area to remove any last bits of silt and mud. Each item is carefully mapped, measured, and photographed before it is moved. Its position may provide clues about how the ship sank and help to identify parts of the ship.

Next, divers place small items in plastic or mesh containers. They use ropes, chains, and pulleys to lift larger items. Air-filled bags may be used to lift very heavy objects. The bags float to the surface and are picked up by crews on boats.

Sometimes archaeologists raise a whole ship to study it or put it on display, which can take many years. When the Swedish ship *Vasa* was raised, divers tunneled under the ship and passed cables through the tunnels. The cables were floated to the surface, carrying the ship with them. The *Mary Rose* was also raised. Its hull was wired to a frame and placed in a cradle. A crane lifted the whole cradle onto a waiting ship.

HOW SCIENCE WORKS
LOCATING SHIPWRECKS

It can be difficult to figure out exactly where a ship sank, especially if it happened long ago. Scientists searching for wrecks use different methods to find them. They may ask fishermen where their nets often get snagged. They search marine archives for records of the ship's last known position. More information may be found in survivors' accounts, if they exist. Once scientists have a good idea of where to start, they use sonar to survey large areas of the seabed. Magnetometers show the location of metal objects, even if they are buried. Debris can be found using cameras like the ones used when searching for the *Titanic*.

FIVE

MAKING SHIPS SAFER

Sailors once relied on lighthouses, charts, and their eyes to avoid dangerous reefs and rocks near shore. Lighthouses were kept burning by a keeper who lived on-site. Lighthouses still warn sailors, but computers, rather than people, usually control them. Floating buoys with lights or foghorns also warn sailors of dangerous coasts.

More important now are tools such as radar, which shows the location of objects even in the dark. Radar equipment works by sending out radio waves and measuring how long it takes them to bounce back, indicating exactly how far away an object is. The Global Positioning System (GPS) has also become very useful.

The U.S. Coast Guard places a buoy to help ships navigate the water.

Beacons and satellites send out signals so ships can easily be tracked.

It uses a network of satellites in space to make it possible for sailors to find their exact location on the globe. It also helps rescuers find survivors when a ship sinks.

HOW GPS WORKS

GPS is made up of a group of satellites that orbit Earth. They send signals to handheld GPS receivers on land, in the air, and at sea. The signals tell the receivers the exact location of the satellite that sent them. The GPS receivers collect signals from many different satellites, and a computer in the receiver then figures out how far away the receiver is from each satellite. The computer can use this information to determine the receiver's precise location on the planet.

New technology helps builders create safer ships. Computer programs let scientists and engineers extensively test their designs to make sure they are safe. New types of steel and other building materials make ships stronger. Ships can also be made safer through new laws. Laws passed after the *Titanic* sank required ships to carry enough lifeboats for all passengers and crew.

RESCUE TECHNOLOGY

Science continues to improve rescue technology, leading to more lives saved. Survival suits can hold body heat in and keep water out. More *Titanic* passengers might have survived with suits like these. Many lifeboats today have roofs to protect passengers from wind and waves. They are stocked with radios, water purifiers, and other survival equipment.

Sometimes the U.S. Coast Guard must perform rescue missions in the water.

Devices called emergency position-indicating radio beacons are now required on certain U.S. vessels. These beacons are activated by water. If a boat sinks, the

beacon sends out information so the U.S. Coast Guard can quickly find the survivors. The coast guard sends planes, helicopters, and boats to the rescue. Helicopter-based rescue swimmers can be lowered by cable to a boat or the water to save lives.

MILITARY DOLPHINS

Underwater mines, bombs that explode when something hits them, can cause great damage to ships. To help locate underwater explosives, navies around the world have trained dolphins and other marine mammals to detect mines in deep, dark waters. Dolphins use their natural sonar, similar to radar, to find mines and other underwater targets. The dolphins leave a device near the mine that marks its location. The animals' handlers can later use this device to find the mine, disarm it, and remove it.

People make mistakes, so it is impossible to prevent all shipwrecks. However, improvements in ship design, navigational tools, safety laws, and rescue equipment have already saved many lives. As we continue to learn from the past, we can use that knowledge to save many more lives following the shipwrecks.

CASE STUDY

THE SINKING OF THE *TITANIC*

Although hundreds of survivors saw the *Titanic* sink, many questions about the condition of the wreck remained. The survivors told very different stories. Some said the ship sank in one piece, but others thought it broke in two. No one knew how much damage the iceberg caused, but most believed it must have torn a huge gash in the ship.

The truth about these questions remained a mystery until Robert Ballard and Jean-Louis Michel discovered the wreck in 1985. Their photos of the site showed that the ship had indeed broken in two. The two halves lay approximately 2,000 feet (600 m) apart on the ocean floor. Although the front looked nearly intact, the back was badly damaged. In 1996, a team of scientists visited the *Titanic* to learn more. They made surprising discoveries. Instead of a long gash, there were only six small slits in the hull, and some were no wider than your finger.

TOP TEN WORST SHIPWRECKS

1. ***WILHELM GUSTLOFF*, 1945**

   A Soviet submarine sank the German ship in 1945 during World War II. More than 9,400 people died.

2. ***GOYA*, 1945**

   Soviet forces sank the *Goya* in 1945. It was carrying wounded troops and civilians. More than 6,800 people died.

3. ***LANCASTRIA*, 1940**

   At least 4,000 people died when the *Lancastria*, a British liner carrying civilians and troops, was bombed by German warplanes in 1940.

4. ***GENERAL VON STEUBEN*, 1945**

   A Soviet submarine sank the *General von Steuben* in 1945. The German ship was carrying injured troops and refugees. As many as 4,500 lives were lost in the wreck.

5. ***DOÑA PAZ*, 1987**

   The *Doña Paz*, a ferry from the Philippines, collided with a tanker ship in 1987. More than 4,300 people were killed.

6. *KIANGYA*, 1948

This Chinese passenger steamship exploded in the mouth of the Huangpu River in 1948. It was carrying many more passengers than it should have been, and up to 3,920 people died.

7. *MONT-BLANC*, 1917

In 1917, the French steamship *Mont-Blanc* collided with another ship in the Halifax harbor and caught fire. When it exploded, 2,000 people died, including people in the nearby city of Halifax, Canada.

8. *LE JOOLA*, 2002

More than 1,800 people died in 2002 when the *Le Joola* ferry capsized off the coast of Gambia. The disaster was blamed on bad weather, poor maintenance, overcrowding, and improper use.

9. *SULTANA*, 1865

The worst shipwreck in U.S. history was the sinking of the *Sultana* on the Mississippi River in 1865. The overloaded steamship was carrying Union prisoners of war back home after the Civil War ended. Approximately 1,700 people died when the ship's boilers exploded.

10. *TEK SING*, 1822

A shortcut proved fatal for the Chinese ship *Tek Sing* in 1822. It struck a reef and sank, leaving approximately 1,600 dead.

GLOSSARY

ARTIFACTS: Objects made by human beings in another era.

BUOYANCY: The force that causes an object to float in a liquid.

BUOYS: Floats marking dangerous waters.

DEPLOYED: Activated and ready for use.

GUN PORTS: The holes in the side of a ship through which cannons fire.

HULL: The shell or body of a ship.

KEEL: The structure on the bottom of a boat that keeps it stable.

MAGNETOMETERS: Instruments for detecting metal objects and magnetic fields.

MARITIME: Relating to the sea and water.

RADARS: Equipment that uses radio waves to locate objects.

REEFS: Ridges of rocks, sand, and coral close to the ocean surface.

SALVAGE: To retrieve items from a shipwreck.

SATELLITES: Objects that move in a curved path around a planet.

SCUBA: Using an air tank and breathing device to dive for long periods of time.

SONAR: A tool for finding underwater objects using sound waves.

FURTHER INFORMATION

BOOKS

Ganeri, Anita and David West. *The Sinking of the Titanic and Other Shipwrecks*. New York: Rosen, 2012.

Stewart, Melissa. *Titanic*. Washington, DC: National Geographic, 2012.

Walker, Sally M. *Secrets of a Civil War Submarine: Solving the Mysteries of the* H. L. Hunley. Minneapolis: Carolrhoda Books, 2005.

WEBSITES

http://www.history.com/interactives/titanic-interactive
This interactive website features information about the design of the *Titanic*, a map of its route, and a timeline of the sinking.

http://www.pbs.org/wgbh/nova/lasalle
This website takes an in-depth look at the sinking of the French ship *La Belle* in 1686. It also has information about buoyancy and the laws regarding shipwrecks.

INDEX